KW

CASH

James Rogers

James Rogers

jim@kwcash.com   www.kwcash.com

ISBN 978-0-9798559-1-7

AXL, Inc. (www.axlinc.com)

Table of Contents

MONEY

Money is a human creation. Anything can be money
if people put a value on it and it is accepted as a
means of exchange. The earliest form of money was
straight one to one barter. Salt, copper, bronze, shells,
gold, silver, rum, tobacco, grains, animals were all
used. Farmers would trade their harvest for animal
skins for example. Barter was inconvenient as you
needed to find someone to accept what you had to
offer.

In 1620 when the Pilgrims landed at Plymouth Rock they brought no money. No gold and silver, no dollar bills, or anything of that sort. How did they conduct transactions among themselves? What kind of money did they use? How did they trade among themselves without money? At first the Colonists used barter. As society grew and became more complex, this arrangement was impractical. One of the innovations was the merchant who opened a general store. He stocked all the things the town might need - cinnamon, sugar, boots, bread, coats, etc. From this, the merchant noticed a certain commodity which had general acceptance in the community and he would accept something such as tobacco as a medium of exchange, or in other words, money. In other places, you might see corn used as money. It all evolved from social norms. All the Colonists had to make this work was the people's agreement and confidence in the medium of exchange.

Money has the following characteristics.

Medium of Exchange. Money avoids the inconveniences of barter. Needs to be easily tradable, transportable, durable, and have liquidity. Anything can back private money. Corn, wheat, rice, fuel, honey, land, etc... Money is an agreement on a medium of exchange. Society needs to accept it.

Unit of Account. It needs to be recognized as valid by all parties. It needs to be divisible without destroying value, and have the same value in different places. It needs to have a specific weight, measure and size.

Standard of value. It must be able to be compare values over time. So money paid today will be valued at some similar measurable form at some time in the future. It can be readily stored and retrieved so that people can save it long term. As such, it needs to be stable and not be inflated away into nothing[i].

We can further divide money in terms of two types - commodity and Fiat. Commodity money itself has intrinsic value. When economies break down people tend to move to money that is commodity backed. Gold, silver, tobacco, tea, corn, jade, rice, etc... Fiat money is backed by some law, government or authority. People accept fiat money because they feel confident they can use it later to purchase what they need. If people lose faith in the government or there is too much fiat money, then the money becomes worthless. We see this during times of trouble such as with the Confederate States, Weimar Germany, China in the 1940's, and now in Zimbabwe. In between these two systems are paper certificates backed by commodities.

For now, if you wish, consider KW Cash as an alternative money system. Alternative currencies are everywhere if you take notice. People will come up with new types of money out of necessity, or fun. If there was a disaster, and the money we use now, had no value, what would you use for money? In some situations, an apple or gallon of water would be worth more than a pound of gold.

During the Banking Panic of 1907, there was a terrible shortage of money in the USA. Instead of general collapse, people found ways to use new forms of money.

Clearinghouse currencies in small denomination were marked "payable through the clearinghouse" and the member banks agreed to accept them. Negotiable cashier's checks were written in 5, 10, or 20 dollar amounts and were payable to some person or entity, "John Smith" or "bearer" or such. These were technically illegal but accepted by the population. Companies paid employees in large numbers of small amounts of scrip. The scrip was the liability of the company issuing it, and was passed from hand to hand as a form of money. Some streetcar companies paid their employees in streetcar tokens and tickets. These circulated well as they had value as streetcar rides.

Alternative currencies will normally be accepted and work quite well if the people agree to use them. In 1907, banks went along with this as it helped to prevent runs on banks. People used alternative currencies and did not need to withdraw so much money from the bank. With a severe shortage of money in the city, people figured out how to deal with the situation. Most of these alternative currencies were illegal. Everyone knew they were illegal, but nobody did anything about it. Part of the reason was the lack of currency, but also, the use was so widespread that the government could not stop it. To bureaucrats and collectivists, this is a nightmare.

1620 to 1913. Money is primarily commodity backed. Most of the money that came into circulation was produced in the form of gold and silver. There were other forms of money in colonial times. Most money is debt free, while debt money is used to finance some commerce.

1913 to 1965. There is a steady shift from debt-free money to debt based money.

1965 to now. Debt free money was killed and close to 100 percent of money is backed by US Government debt.

Soon – later in the 21st Century. New money systems backed by kilowatt hours. This ends when energy is extremely abundant.

KW MONEY AS A MEDIUM OF EXCHANGE

KW Cash is money that is backed by kilowatt hours.
Electricity reaches into nearly every home and business in the country. It is used by everyone and once
we figure out a way to make credits used as easily as
money, KW Cash, will become a very strong medium
of exchange. Electricity and energy backed money
will be spent among the general population. Once we
can find a way to make it easy, people will spend
these energy credits everyday.

It is money that can be produced by anyone and is regulated by the government. Until about 2000, this was impractical due to technical issues. Now, technology allows us to use smart card and information technology to track all the energy.

Imagine a time in the future if the money collapses, or there is a disaster. What will be more useful for you - gold coins or a generator, car, fuel and sustainable system that will give you power. If the situation is dire, how far will that gold get you. If you are a savvy negotiator, you will no doubt do very well. However, most people will spend the metals away, and the money will be hoarded by a few astute groups. On the other hand, a generator, and fuel can run water filters, a greenhouse in cold climates, provide heat and light. You can also barter this with others, and spend this energy into the economy.

Prior to the 19th Century most energy came from the sun, flowing streams, and biomass – wood and waste. Prior to the 20th Century most work was done with muscle power. We see terms like horsepower, etc... With the industrial revolution and the steam engine, our living standards have risen. The advances we have made through history correlates with the amount of energy which we harness and use. With the growth of cars, people moved to the suburbs. Now with the internet, people can work from anywhere.

Electric power transformed our lives. To a large extent, electricity defines modern technological civilization. The reasons may not be easy to appreciate for those who have never known the filth, toil, and danger associated with obtaining and using such fuels as wood, coal, and whale oil. Now, electricity is clean, flexible, controllable, safe, effortless, and instantly available. In homes, it runs everything from toothbrushes and televisions to heating and cooling systems. Outdoors, electricity guides traffic, aircraft, and ships, and lights up the night. Electricity is an essential part of our life. Just look at the problems we suffer during ice storms and blackouts. Lack of heating and air conditioning can cause death during extreme weather.

Electricity is essential to our future industries – medical, computer, telecom, etc...

Medical equipment, pace makers, machines

Ambulances, helicopters – medical evacuations.

Electricity is still young in the grand scheme of things. Information technology and electricity are born from the same parent, fundamental energy. These two sides will brings us smart energy, or the smart grid.

1950 – 2000. Population growth. 89 percent. Electricity Growth 1300 percent.

1900 – 2MW plant

1903 – 5MW plant

1905 – 18MW plant

1912 – 35MW plants

1953 - 125 MW plants

1967 – 1000 MW plants

The United States is the wealthiest country in the world. A huge part of the wealth is the energy production and consumption. Fossil fuels have been the key reason. Oil, gas and coal are the big three that have powered the nation. We see a strong relationship between growth in GDP and supply of electricity.

Many states are mandating that the utilities cooperation with people who make extra energy, though net-metering arrangements. Instead of a headache, this can turn into a massive profit machine. For one thing, utilities can focus on distribution and transmission of electricity, and let go aging coal powered plants. Utilities set up the framework for the transactions to take place, deliver energy and make sure that everyone gets paid. Absolutely, from a profit standpoint the utilities will be the biggest winners as they will control the transactions and set up systems to promote more electricity.

Banks and financial clearing houses can earn excellent rates, as once the system is set up they collect transaction fees of every delivery. Banks can also take distressed properties, develop renewable energy sources and mix the output in with traditional money.

Software companies such as SAP, IBM, Oracle and so forth will earn excellent returns. They can earn transaction fees if they so desire. Smaller companies will be able to get niche markets and set up virtual power plants with payment made in KW Cash.

Retailers will find ways to build in viral marketing campaigns, coupons, databases, incentives and so forth

Inventors can earn royalties in KW Cash.

Consumers will love this as they can have a myriad of options

Entrepreneurs will fan out looking for opportunities to convert stuff into energy. They will find fields, desert, farms, you name it

Farmers and Ranchers can add power to their land and then earn currency as offsets or where they can sell to others. **Other land owners** can lease their land out and earn higher rents. Likewise investors buy land, place equipment on it and they earn income.

Leasing companies can place equipment on land and then get payment in KW Cash. **Manufacturers** can finance the equipment all with electric output if they so wish.

Employers can be part of this and add this as an employee benefit. Employees can get some extra pay in KW Cash arbitrarily, or based on certain programs in place like charging up at work, V2G, green energy programs and so forth

States. States have the resources, land, and people. A state could wipe out its own debt and add funds to pensions with energy backed KW Cash. **Local Governments** can allocate land for energy production and then earn this as income. They can export energy to surrounding states, counties etc..

Military. The logistics requirements of fuel are difficult in remote locations. Vehicles on the battlefield will provide the power for new laser weapon systems.

State and private pensions systems can offer this as an investment option to workers. The worker will place a certain amount in the fund and then at retirement they will get paid back with monthly energy credits. Imagine getting 100 MWH every month to spread around, sell or accrue.

KW MONEY AS A UNIT OF ACCOUNT

Money needs to be recognized as valid by all parties. It needs to be divisible without destroying value, and have the same value in different places. It needs to have a specific weight (or amount), measure and size. Gold and silver fit this very well, and now kilowatt hours can do the same.

When representatives from the newly independent United States of America met to draft a Constitution, they decided to standardize the money. Congress would decide on how money was made and measured which would help trade among the States.

In the U.S. Constitution, Article I, Section 8,

"Congress shall have power to coin money, regulate the value there of"

The Founders knew the flaws caused by a fiat currency and looked for a suitable commodity backed money. They chose silver. In 1792 George Washington signed the Coinage Act which determined the exact composition of the dollar. Silver was the primary unit of measure and gold was derived from its relation to silver.

	Dollars	Gold	Silver
		grains	grains
Eagles	10.00	247.500	
½ Eagles	5.00	123.750	
¼ Eagles	2.50	61.875	
Dollars	1.00		371.250
½ Dollars	0.50		185.625
¼ Dollars	0.25		92.812
Dimes	0.10		37.125
Nickels	0.05		18.587

Gold and silver specifications

Note: 1 ounce = 437.5 grains and one pound = 7000 grains

1 troy ounce = 480 grains

^ Calculated using the relationship:

1 troy ounce = 31.1034768 grams

The term used for gold coins was EAGLES, and the EAGLES had a relative value to the dollar.

The laws were focused on the weights and measures of the money. The government was there to provide a service to mint coins and ensure there was a common value. They opened up the minting of silver to all people, and allowed foreign coins to be used. People could take the silver to a mint where it was coined into very exact sizes, weights and mixed with exact amounts of alloys. Anyone could go out and dig up gold and silver, or conduct trade to attain silver, then bring it to a mint to be coined. The first mint was established in Philadelphia in 1792 and we now have mints in San Francisco (1854), Denver (1906), and

West Point (1973). It was too troublesome to ship the gold to Philadelphia to mint so the Government also had mints established in Charlotte, North Carolina (1838–1861) and Dahlonega, Georgia (1838–1861) to mint local gold deposits into gold coins. Andrew Jackson set up a mint in New Orleans, (1838– 1909) to help people in the South and West. It minted gold and silver in all denominations. Carson City (1870 - 1893) was set up primarily for silver coins. There have been private mints especially during gold rushes. These private mints would coin gold or silver to US specifications and the money was circulated just as if the Government did minted the coins.

In 1792, the proportional value of gold and silver as 15 units of pure silver to 1 unit of pure gold. Standard gold was defined as 11 parts pure gold to one part al-loy composed of silver and copper. As long as both were used for money there was a natural ratio of sil-ver and gold. Over time, there were some adjustments made to the coinage to account for changes in the balance of international trade. Still,

Congress was able to control itself because it worked within the constraints of gold and silver. There was some inflation and deflation in the money, but over-all, the money stayed pretty consistent in value over a long period of time.

	Dollar (grains silver)	Eagle (grains gold)	Silver: Gold
April 2, 1792	371.25	247.5	15 to 1
June, 1834	371.25	232	16 to 1
Jan. 18, 1837	206.25	258	8 to 1
Feb. 12, 1873	378	258	14.6 to 1

Even until 1857 foreign gold and silver coins were allowed as legal money.

Anyone could bring in silver, and government put it into a form that all of the economy could agree upon.

Congress can establish money that has energy as its backing. This falls in line with the strict weights and measures that we saw back in 1792. People can use it as a barter tool to regulate value. States could set up currency systems with energy backing, though they may need to trick the system to mix in come gold and silver. This would satisfy the demands of the Constitution. States can cover deficits, provide it like food stamps, or simply establish it and call it something besides money. Another way would be to mix in some money that has a little bit of silver added to it.

Let's talk about the weights and measures. Energy is the capacity to do work or transfer heat. Power is doing that in a period of time. Here are the units of measure.

Energy Units	Power is Energy Flow
Kilowatt Hour	Kilowatts
Calorie	Calories/minute
BTU	BTU/second or BTU/hour
joule	joule/sec = watt
Horsepower hour	Horsepower/hour

Each of these measures is convertible to the other.

BTU	British Thermal Unit -- One BTU can raise the temperature of one pound of water one degree Fahrenheit (°F)
Cal	Large or kilogram calorie -- One Cal can raise the temperature of one kilogram of water one degree Celsius (°C)
cal	small or gram calorie -- One cal can raise one gram of water one degree Celsius
ft-lb	The energy exerted by a force of one pound moving one foot
KW-hr	The energy it takes to run a 1000 watt appliance or light for one hour
joule	The energy exerted by a force of one newton moving one meter

Here are some technical conversions.

1 joule = 0.239 calories (cal)

1 calorie = 4.187 joules (J)

1 British thermal unit (Btu) = 1055 joules

1 Quad = 1000 trillion Btu or approximately
172 million barrels of oil equivalent (boe)

Power

1 watt = 1.0 joule/second = 3.413 Btu/hr

1 kilowatt (kW) = 3413 Btu/hr = 1.341 horsepower

1 MW (mW) = 1,341 horsepower

1 kilowatt-hour (KWH) = 3.6 MJ = 3413 Btu

1 horsepower (hp) = 550 foot-pounds per second = 2545 Btu per hour = 745.7 watts =
0.746 kW

FUEL

Oil prices will continue to rise. Transportation uses two-thirds of all the oil used.

Diesel gallon	41.420 KWH
Gasoline gallon	36.718 KWH
LNG gallon	27.316 KWH
Propane gallon	26.687+/-1.703 KWH
Ethanol gallon	23.091 KWH
Methanol gallon	17.413 KWH

Bio-fuels are ideal as fuels to support KW Cash. They come from the energy of the sun, so they are renewed yearly. They have the potential to replace crude oil and help with the trade deficit. Bio-diesel can replace diesel 100 percent while ethanol can replace up to 85 percent of gasoline. Biofuels give better engine performance and less pollution. Oil and coal have sulfur, while biofuels have none. They have less CO2 emissions which should appeal to a lot of people. Some biofuels are made from garbage, sewage, and other wastes.   Along with this, biofuel plants can be small in size so that farms, towns and cities can set up their own production.

Gasoline	12 KWH/kg
Wood	3.154+/-1.554 KWH/kg
Secondary Lithium-Ion	0.11 KWH/kg
Lead Acid Battery	0.025 KWH/kg
Nickel Metal Hydride	0.06 KWH/kg
Flywheel	0.12 KWH/kg
Storage capacitors	0.5 to 10 W·h/kg
Ice to water	0.0093 KWH/kg

The best government role is to set standards, and set up a legally supported framework. Production and economic growth comes from the private sector economy. We move to a private money production system that is government supported and regulated, not with government restrictions and synthetic monopolies.

KW MONEY AS A STANDARD OF VALUE

This is the key challenge and roadblock to using kilowatt hours as money. Electricity is used instantly and is very expensive to store. Clearly gold and silver are superior in this regard, as they can last 1000 years. So, we need to think in some ways to make this work.

The price of electricity in terms of dollars is going up up up. The inflation started around the early 1970s and has gone up about four percent each year.

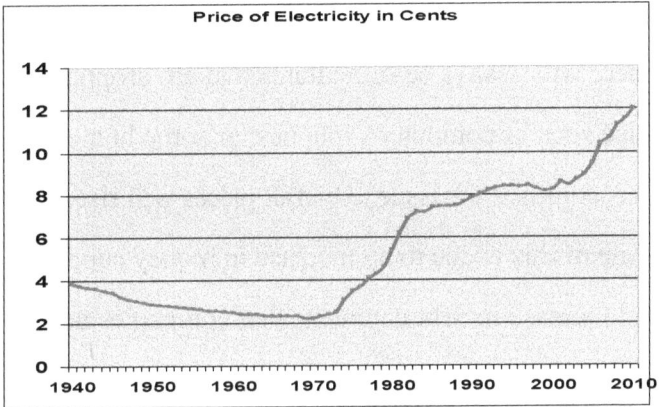

Price of Electricity in Cents

Electricity in cents

Who has not seen the prices of gasoline, food, housing, and such items increase over time? Chocolate bars were a nickel and now a dollar. With a dollar you could buy a coffee and the Sunday newspaper.

This translates into gold prices. This is the benefit to owning precious metals like gold and silver. It is not that the gold or silver is getting more valuable, rather there is a flood of new paper money on the market, and the value of each paper dollar is getting less and less. If you own gold or silver, in a few decades, you will have maintained some level of wealth.

There will always be some items that are dropping in price such as computers, iphones, or some homes. This confuses the issue. Overall prices will rise, and some of this is due to an increase in money supply and increase in debt payments that companies need to pass onto consumers.

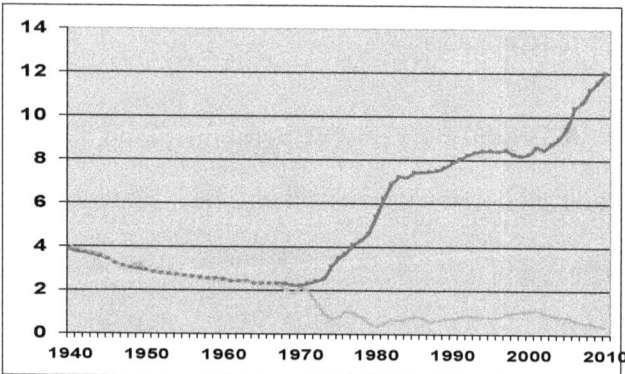

Electricity and Gold

In terms of gold, the price of electricity is quite steady. It is the depreciation of the dollar that is the issue here. In fact, electricity in terms of gold or silver gets a little bit cheaper each year, reflecting the technology aspect that is similar to other technology in our lives – phone, computers, etc...

TECHNICAL ISSUES

KW Money is designed to work within the existing financial and energy systems. There are unlimited revenue and pricing models. Secure, trusted tools manage the relationships between consumers, suppliers, and service providers. All kids of plans can be put together. Transactions tie in with the energy management systems.

A wide range of service providers participate. Agents and third parties produce, distribute and provide information or transaction services. These provide customers with access to range of suppliers and producers from multiple sources. They use some means to identify and group customers according to class, location, etc... An agent's business model will let it add a premium as they are bringing economies of scale and provided services to the marketplace. They add efficiencies, guarantees, financing, and pull together groups to bring in discounts.

Service providers will be a very important part of the growth of this process. They open many new business models, push viral marketing and build the exponential growth. In addition to the financial aspects, there are all kinds of data applications here. These are tied in with marketing, vehicle use, media, telecom, and endless other applications. Marketing related information tied to demographic, income, and other factors are used. These can add new levels of opportunities for incentives, and discounts. These also bring about schemes for bundling. For example, an air conditioner is sold with a set amount of kilowatts that are financed. Groups of individuals can come together in a peer to peer method to form a buying group. Imagine some of the capabilities of Groupon.

There are great opportunities for software companies, consulting companies and any sort of service provider. They not only will figure out great ways to bring these to the market but they will be able to have an extra layer that gets transaction revenue. This will provide long term steady income

Kilowatt Cash supports an unlimited number of revenue and pricing models. This is done through deploying a set of secure, trusted applications, and tools that support the commerce. These manage the relationships between consumers, suppliers, and service providers.

Suppliers. KW Cash provides security and management capabilities that let owners, suppliers, distributors of energy sources, bring their energy to the marketplace. Numerous niche markets and schemes can be developed. Service providers. KW Cash also adds capabilities that let service providers become part of the chain. Rules such as permissions, rights, financial and amounts. Providers can bring to market clearing accounts, cards, membership schemes, etc… Services including customer support, payments, management and third party efficiencies.

Pricing strategies can include subscription, pay per use, pay per time interval, prices that decline over time, usage prices, usage prices up to a limit, volume discounts, suite discounts, and upgrade and sale discounts. Downstream rightsholders like distributors can, subject to senior rightsholder constraints, add new controls that augment or modify earlier controls.

Service participation. As needed, a wide range of service providers, including financial, rights and permissions, and usage data clearinghouses, Identity Producerities, and software and hardware implementers, can participate in value chains.

In a four-component process:

1 Secures transaction information including usage rules, usage data, payment data, and amounts.

2 A tamper resistant software and or hardware that makes the contents act in accordance with the business rules. Administrative rules and consequences governing the use of content, including metering, permission, and pricing information;

3 A means to allow the device to transmit and communicate though any medium such as POTS, ATM, TCPIP, wireless, direct access, etc.

4 Send payment and usage records to third party data centers for processing, reporting and acknowledgement. Usage data created for

outflow purposes, including reporting, advertising, and market analysis. Payment records together with related information that tells payment processors about the amounts, payer, merchant, and other information required to complete the payment transactions.

Bank and financial clearinghouses

The system is compatible with nearly any payment method, from credit cards, paypal, to corporate billing services, to automated clearinghouses for funds transfer and direct deposit, to EDI transactions. Rightsholders and other value chain participants will be able to choose the set of potential payment methods they wish to enable for a given property.

A common clearinghouse strategy will be to provide an interface to established payment services, using the buyer's secure, locally stored kilowatt currency or units.

At specified times, the software or hardware device will communicate with a financial clearinghouse. It will report accumulated usage and purchase records, and optionally replenish locally stored units. The business rules may be set by the utility, producer, distributor or government and adjusted according to business rules.

Key point: Now computing power is strong enough to handle enormous amounts of transactions of micropayments quickly, accurately and at a low cost. The clearinghouse will gather together the buy side and sell side transactions and settle the accounts in real time or batch mode.

This ability allows stakeholders to create new business models, revenue flows, and forms of relationships to better serve customers. This also brings new efficiencies and financial instruments.

Clearinghouse services will resemble those of credit card companies and we can expect over time that the fee structure will be somewhat similar – being in the 2 to 5 percent range.   These funds are then subdivided between participating financial service entities, which can include:

Clearinghouse with or without help from a card processing company

Bank that handles funds

Computers and communications to support.

Data

In addition to the financial aspects there are also inventory, location, and other types of data. Solar energy will be influenced by time of day, and year; wind energy affected by wind conditions, etc… Likewise consumer and business data will accrue vast amounts of data that can be used for forecasting. As plug-in hybrids and electric cars enter the market, these will greatly influence data issues.

Data can cover such things as usage data by time of

day, appliance, car, etc. The car usage can be mobile as the kilowatts can be transacted using a credit card like device or built in with the car.

Rules can follow appliances.

These can add new levels of opportunities for incentives, and discounts.

These also bring about schemes for bundling. For example, an air conditioner can be sold with a set amount of kilowatts that are transacted and accounted for. Likewise such financing schemes for plug-in or electric cars can be numerous in scope, size and type.

Peak usage can be addressed as time of day usage can be programmed into the various hardware and software.

Marketing related information tied to demographic, income, and other factors can be factored.

The data can be very valuable and used in developing new efficiencies in the market. The clearinghouses that collect this data can analyze and provide to others for income or efficiencies. Likewise business rules that protect consumer data can be put into effect.

Established permissions are a key part of the success of this process. Groups of individuals can come together in a peer to peer method to form a buying group to negotiate group buying and selling. Some permissions will be assigned by government, utilities and some will be voluntary as in a commercial transaction. Likewise the entity that assigns permissions can earn ongoing micropayments on a time based, or transaction basis. This is particularly applicable for taxation.

NETWORKING MODELS

The networking technology needed for future electricity grids already exists. There is still some work or inventions needed to make the actual low voltage power lines safer and cheaper, but that think of all the technical innovations once new markets grow. The data and accounting systems are far beyond what we need. Banking ATM networks can deliver cash on demand worldwide. Phone apps, instant messaging, MSN, Yahoo Messenger, and such can add new functionality.

Online multi-player games can handle millions of people at a time, all interacting with the game engine and other people. Developing these games and running them requires deep skills in handling complex networks, audits, accounting and technology. The online gaming industry requires large data centers full of hundreds or thousands of computers and networks. The younger generation is very open to new forms of currency. All kinds of game currency (weapons, characters, and digital cash) are traded in virtual currency. They make it, trade it, and use it. Online games like Second Life combine real world money with virtual worlds. People barter among virtual currencies and use real money to buy virtual money.

BUSINESS MODELS

Let's look at a few business models from least to greater complexity.

Most basic level. At this level, it is just the customer and another customer, or the utility. The customer may have an electric vehicle, own power supply, or live entirely off the grid. They may deploy some batteries to buy cheap energy at night and go off grid during the peak expensive periods.

At the most basic level two nodes representing end users can communicate and conduct a transaction. They would exchange at least two messages related to negotiation of an energy supply from one to the other.

With this transaction, energy can flow from one to the other. The messages will be in a standard format such as EDI or XML.

The first scenario is a simple one – a direct transaction where a customer has a direct link to the source of energy. They will use a clearinghouse to manage the transaction. The clearinghouse is tied in with the utility.

Revenue Pricing Model One

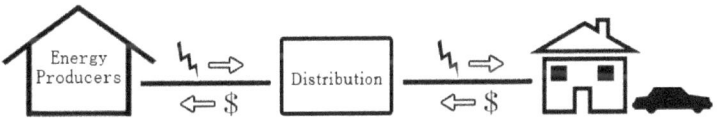

This simple model shows electricity and money each going in one direction. Here the energy producer gets 77 percent of the revenue, and the various other participants get 23 percent.

Energy Producer	77%	
Utility	10%	
3rd Part	5%	
Info Tech Provider	5%	
Local Tax	2%	
Tax	1%	

These splits are arbitrary and changed however the parties wish. Then in terms of raw KWH numbers we split things out below.

	50 KWH	Service Providers	Tax	
Participants				
Energy Producer	38.5	2.5	1	
Utility	5			
3rd Part	2.5		0.5	
Total	46	2.5	1.5	**50**

The various business rules added (e.g. pricing, time, importance criteria, min/max, and limits) by the energy supplier, energy management system and the users will let all parties to optimize and negotiate benefits to both sides.

Now let's take it further and add in a whole range of agents. These can be appliance manufacturers, stores, coffee shops, car dealers and on and on. Maybe they subscribe to an organization such as a credit card company, or non-profit organization. The agent will claim a portion as markup.

Local level. In a group of homes on a street, or small neighborhood, the participants will buy and sell from each other. When there is a shortage, some local resources can kick in, such as a car or generator. The transactions stay local. It can tap into the small energy sources at customer's homes and vehicles. The local transformer will distributed power within its network, and the transactions are accounted locally.

This will open up new capacity for electric automobiles to recharge while absorbing potential strain on the power grid. Electric energy companies will achieve better efficiencies. They will save investment costs on existing poles, wires, stations and plants. They will have more new sources of high profit revenue as they broker energy transactions. This will help to relieve power grid bottlenecks and constraints.

Revenue Pricing Model Two

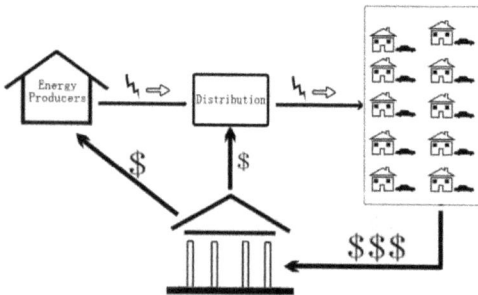

We start with a similar share as before, but there are more parties to take taxes or fees for services.

Energy Producer	77%
Utility	10%
3rd Party	5%
Info Tech Provider	3%
Agent	2%
Local Tax	2%
National Tax	1%

So as we convert these percentages out among the players, we come up with the followingKW Cash.

Participants	80 KWH	Service Pro-viders		Tax	
Energy Producer	61.6	Info Tech	2.4	1.6	
Utility	8	Agent	1.6		
3rd Party	4			0.8	
Total	73.6		4	2.4	80

The transactions are as simple or as complex as the parties want. Homeowners, business owners, and service providers set up their own preferences. All the communications and programming are set up by computer companies, utilities and others. A financial clearinghouse comes in to make sure that all participants are compensated.

This level of commerce would not take too much time to establish. Within a few years, we can see this in operation. Vehicle to grid operations, small towns, remote communities, and all sorts of other scenarios can use this simple model.

As mentioned earlier, all kinds of third parties can get involved and drive these revenue models. In fact, it makes sense for some IT entrepreneurs to set up these simple systems. They will be able to tap into two of the biggest industries we have – energy and finance.

Applications are endless. Long-term regulated agreements are put in place to provide incentives to buy electric powered cars and renewable energy. The business rules can also apply to the communications and screen for other like-minded participants.

Let's look at a model which has more emphasis on third party agents.

Revenue Pricing Model Three

This figure shows how numerous agents may be included in a transaction. The payment is split among an energy producer, utility, agent, 4th parties and multiple sources at some of these levels.

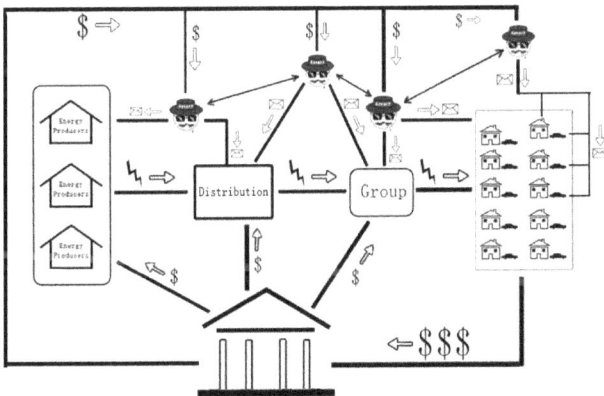

The Agent contacts get a request to fill an energy need and contacts the customer. They have a previous agreement in place that could cover any range of parameters, like selling during peak demand and buying during dips. So the communication between them goes back and forth - contact, negotiate and confirm. Many times this will be computers and machines talking to other computers and machines based on established agreements already in place.

The data is valuable and used in developing new efficiencies in the market. The clearinghouses that collect this data can analyze and provide to others for income or efficiencies. The table shows how a data clearinghouse can profit from handling and processing data.

Energy Producer	77%
Utility	10%
3rd Party	5%
Info Tech Provider	2%
Agent	1%
Financial company	1%
Data Company	1%
Local Tax	2%
National Tax	1%

Town level. We start to see virtual power plants. If you take a large number of small systems and make them appear and act as one larger power plant then you have a virtual power plant. In this environment, all the pieces are virtualized and combined to look like one larger resource.

Membership in groups comes into play now and adds to viral marketing and the spread of KW Cash transactions. Membership could have discounts for classes like retirees or veterans or alumni, political affiliation, common ideals, religion, sports teams, newspaper subscribers.

130KWH					
Participants		Service Providers	Tax		
Energy Producer	100.1	I.T.	2.6	2.6	
Utility	13	Agent	1.3		
3rd Party	6.5	Financial company	1.3	1.3	
		Data Company	1.3		
Total	119.6		6.5	3.9	130

Membership Cards protects the proper use of discounts, improves distribution efficiency, and improves the customer's ease-of-use. Agents and vendors that use these pay an additional service charge or receive payment as determined in the business rules.

County, State Level. Here we see larger networks and Virtual Power Plants. Whole robust communities will evolve. Each location can have a number of power generating devices, and each of those have a unique identification. For example, a small business has a solar array, wind turbine, battery packs and some vehicles with batteries. There can also be many nodes in remote areas such as a wind farm or solar concentrator. Then as two or more join they can have one time or long term relationships and transactions. Once the other sources are identified then the users swap or transact energy.

People within a P2P network create connections with others forming a group of two or more. Applications are endless. Group systems set up where people opt into a virtual network of energy users and savers that use a series of business rules to swap or trade energy back and forth.

We have seen Peer-to-peer networks expand very quickly. Technology will drive breakthroughs that make local power generation cheaper and more convenient. What is new is the emerging trend for individuals to become power producers and owners of the means to produce, then to share these resources with others. The optimization will reach across many owners and make the overall system more robust and secure.

Peer to peer is not so new. There were earlier sorts of applications. Car dealers have had peer to peer commerce systems for decades. They are able to locate parts and order directly from other car dealers. Car Dealer A could send out a parts request to a local network of dealers and quickly get an answer of availability, price and delivery time. This was first put into work in the 80's and was standard practice for car dealers in the USA in the 1990's. The communications to make this happen went through a central hub, and though expensive by today's standards, it worked very well and was big business. Without this, the parts departments would rely on phone calls and higher inventory amounts. The vendor provided a valuable service and was rewarded very well.

The direct buying and selling of power will also free up space on the traditional large transmission lines, as buyers and sellers can deliver over local power networks. A lot of these networks will need to be set up from scratch, but that is part of the whole economic growth model.

Energy distribution will be more dispersed and rely less on large power plants at the ends of the energy supply chain. The slack in the end of the power grid can absorb enormous additional capacity that could not occur in a top down centralized approach as we now have. This will be especially useful in blackouts, ice storms, and disaster situations. A distributed grid resists a military attack against the power grid. It would be much harder to take down the entire grid if the bottlenecks have multiple workarounds and backups. It can help to isolate problems and thus provide fault containment that would not be possible otherwise.

Each virtual environment is managed and developed from scratch. There are many environments, from a small two node system, to something that takes place nationwide. It can be industry groups, affiliations, sports teams' promotions, coffee shops, chain stores, and peer to peer networks, anything...

There will be many applications that tie into other forms of entertainment and parts of our lives. Think what sports can do to leverage their brands into fabulous multiplayer games. Also, with new technology like 3D TV, holograms home entertainment complexes, the electricity required will be huge. This grows the use of electricity, builds wealth and creates jobs.

Energy Producer	77%
Utility	10%
3rd Party	5%
Info Tech Provider	1%
Agent	0.5%
Financial company	1%
Data Company	1%
Member/Clubs	1%
Services Companies	0.5%
Local Tax	2%
National Tax	1%

This will lead to great incentives for energy production, and promotion among users. There are two main processes here (1) the information sharing and negotiation and (2) the financial transaction This level can hand off the data and transaction to a third party that provides clearing services for the transaction. This third party can be the utility or a software company.

	200 KWH	Service Providers		Tax	
Energy Producer	154	Info Tech	2	4	
Utility	20	Agent	1		
3rd Party	10	Financial company	2	2	
		Data Company	2		
		Member/Clubs	2		
		Services Co.	1		
Total	184		10	6	200

After the contract there are reporting structures in place on service performance, variances and delivery. The transactions are automated by rules and artificial intelligence.

The various business rules added (e.g. pricing, time, importance criteria, min/max, and limits) by the energy supplier, energy management system and the users will let all parties optimize and negotiate benefits to both sides. This provides new areas of optimization at the user level, group level or across the entire grid. This allows mass personalization of decisions and also at the higher level for inventory of energy to be gathered and optimized across a wide area.

Superdistribution

Superdistribution models let customers become redistributors. This ties in very well with the grouping method and recruiting drives that can spur renewable energy. Customers can become group leaders and earn overrides on transactions. They can also develop multi-level models of sales and distribution. The following shows how this might work.

Superdistribution concept has been around for 20 years. Japanese professor Ryoichi Mori at the Institute of Information Sciences and Electronics looked proposed that people could forward electronic content to others so they could try before they buy. Then they would have a mechanism in place to get paid automatically and securely. The interests of all the participants are protected. No firm agreement is needed and the change of money is automatic for all parties.

As applied here, the electric content is the information and financial transactions. The electricity is sent and delivered through the electric grid or newer smart micro-grids. The information and transactions are matched with the actual delivery through computer programming and accounting systems.

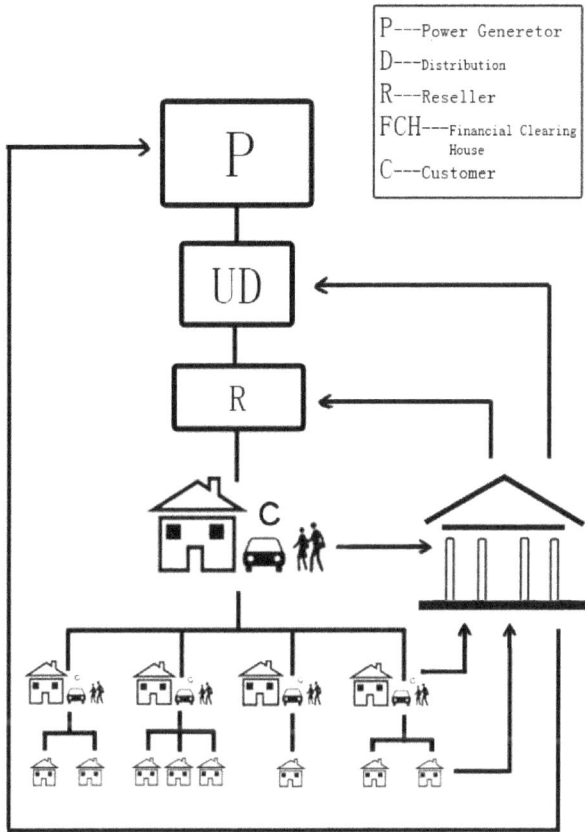

P---Power Generetor
D---Distribution
R---Reseller
FCH---Financial Clearing House
C---Customer

Let's dream of a scenario where this can happen with KW Cash. An unleashed distributed power network could see enormous growth in energy. With an annual growth rate that is very moderate by internet standards, we could see:

- double installed electricity capacity by 2020 and double again by 2030.
- cut pollution 50 to 90 percent from present levels
- cut out all oil imports to a negligible level and start to export energy again.

SCENARIO

Here is a breakdown for a new car sale. Someone
buys a new electric or hybrid car. That car needs 400
watts per mile. They buy a package that gives them
15000 miles over the next forty years, which is the
expected life of the wind turbine. This is financed for
the first twenty years and the second twenty years is
all theirs to keep.

15000 miles X 400 watts per mile is 6000
KWH need each year, or 500 each month.

6000 KWH needs 2 KWH capacity

Each KWH of capacity costs 5000 dollars, so they will need a loan for 10,000 dollars.

Using a 20 year loan at one percent interest, we get monthly payments of 46 dollars.

500 KWH each month costing 12 cents is worth 60 dollars so they have a nice 14 dollar benefit there. As electricity prices go up in the future, this benefit increases.

So in this deal, the new car owner would have a monthly payment of 46 dollars over the next twenty years, as opposed to 60 dollars. Any KWH the car owner does not use is used as money in the form ofKW Cash. Any time the owner is short of KWH in any month, he can buy from the electric grid.

This is a better system than taxation. It would stir the market and provide the financing. Compare this to the current situation where money is hard to raise and there are all sorts of hands in the cookie jar.

Now the government taxes you, then borrows from the Federal Reserve and adds to the national debt. Finally, they come back to you to pay the interest on the national debt. The government says they will issue grants to research and development for developing the turbines and other items. That grant money comes from the budget which must be borrow from the banks, and back to the debt which ultimately is paid by the taxpayer. At all points, there is debt and taxes.

A better way is to have public works projects that are privately financed. The government is a support for the private economy instead of the private economy supporting bureaucrats and usurers.

This can also be done with homeowners. They use the same calculations we went through with cars.

You replace miles with home energy use and bundle the payment in with the mortgage payment.

Universities

Universities can set up funding mechanisms. Parents buy into the energy with the savings plans. Then they pay tuition in the future with amounts on order of 10 MW per year, fixed. The invested amount goes into wind farms, and micro grids. Students earn credits for doing things for the community, care for the elderly, etc... The schools can set aside a quota of 5 percent or so to cash in these currency units. Online education communities can useKW Cash to facilitate barter. The professors can accept money in LETS hours, Federal Reserve debt money, orKW Cash. The students can pay likewise.

Scenario – Year 2030.

Most cars have advanced battery storage capacity holding far more than needed to offload onto the grid. As coal fired plants age, they are shut down.

The town has developed more than enough energy for its own needs. They have three GWH generating capacity. From this they use one GWH; they export and sell one GWH capacity, which brings in millions of dollars to its tax base, and use the other GWH as incentives. The residents who bought into the coop get dividends and rebates from this as well as eliminating their power bill. Due to recent economic changes, the town decided to attract companies with high wage jobs with very attractive rates to the company on power, subsidies and land use. The city issues bonds backed and guaranteed by the MWH sales contracts that it has developed with buyers. These bonds are used for infrastructure, arts, and general welfare.

The downtown area has one million square feet of commercial office space and power systems they use an array of distributed resources. They fill up on energy during early morning hours and place this potential into banks of flywheels, batteries and such storage.

Then vehicles in the parking lot can plug in and help with peak load, base load or even sell their KWH to neighboring buildings. The hybrid cars can turn on engines and feed power right into the local grid and work as an emergency generators in times of blackout, or unusual peak demand. As an added benefit, this CHP system also will provide a significant benefit to the City distribution grid by reducing load on the grid during the critical summer peak hours.

It plans to tie in the parking garage so that BEV and PHEV can offload KWH of energy during peak times. This energy will be paid back to the customer in credits. The office town pulled in their parking garage to installs a system for pulling KWH from the cars and selling to the local buildings. The garage has 1000 slots, 400 of which are able to pull in KWH. In exchange for 10KWH, they reduce the price of parking by half. This provides 4 MWH per cay - 400 x 10 KWH - during peak times.

A major franchise retail store decides to promote clean energy as part of its corporate social responsibility. They offer clean KWH credits to their customers.

These credits are used as cash. The customers use this as gifts or make purchases at other locations. The store opens a membership club. A percentage of sales from customers go into a membership pool for renewable energy. The store keeps half and the customers get credit for their proportion. The more they purchase, the more they get credits.

This nationwide retail store sets up a remote site for low cost concentrated solar power of more than 100 MW installed capacity and some wind energy shares. Each store installs PV cells, small wind and battery banks. Excess power is sold to customers who have PHEV and come to the store to shop. They are given free KWH if they buy more than 50 dollars in any one trip. If the stores, cannot fulfill their energy requirements then they buy from the grid at prevailing rates. At nighttime they load up on cheap base load energy, and use that during the day.

ENDNOTES

---

[i] Pulled from multiple sources…   Andrew Carnegie, US Government, Textbooks